W9-AEC-047

ADVENTURE AT THE TOP OF THE WORLD

By SHELLEY GILL   Photos by J.T. LINDHOLM
and JENNIFER JOHNSTON

Jennifer and Merrick mumble, pack, discard, pack, argue, pack. It all has to fit and it all has to be there.

Merrick Johnston carried a rock to the top of the world. It was a gift from her good friend, Norman Vaughan, who brought it from the top of a mountain at the bottom of the world. This very small rock came to symbolize a very big dream.

At 12 years old, Merrick Johnston wanted to be the youngest person to ever reach the summit of Denali, (Mt. McKinley) the tallest peak in North America.

Rising 20,320 feet into the frigid air of Alaska, Denali is a serious mountain--no place for wimps or amateurs. A lot of people have died here; some have lost fingers and feet to frostbite. Others have fallen to their deaths in crevasses or been crushed by avalanches. Still others have simply disappeared, blown away or buried forever to become legends of what Alaskans simply call "The Mountain." Each section of the West Buttress route that Merrick planned to climb revealed the heart of the snow covered stone: Windy Corner, Rescue Gulch, the Valley of Death, Heartbreak Hill.

Merrick's team included her mom Jennifer, Danielle Carvalho, Breck Eagle, J.T. Lindholm, Jani Oviatte, assistant guide Chuck Landry and guide Steve Young. All together they were known as Acey Deucy and The Cribheads.

Day 1 June 2, 1995 Base Camp

The team flew to Base Camp from Talkeetna, Alaska, elevation 300 feet. At 7000 feet, Base Camp on the Kahiltna Glacier is a small tea cup surrounded by giant marshmallow mountains: Mt. Hunter, Mt. Francis, Mt. Foraker and Denali. Merrick amused herself by doing back flips wearing her heavy climbing boots. An accomplished gymnast, Merrick began this climb after a year of training: hiking, running and climbing. But being in good shape was no guarantee she would make it up the mountain. Some good climbers can't make to the top; and some never make it down. The first big mountain under Merrick's belt was 10,654 foot Mt. Goode, located in Southcentral Alaska. She and her mother spent two days on that one. They would spend the next 26 days on Denali. Merrick spent Day 1 setting up camp, eating the first meal of freeze-dried food and sleeping, for the first time, with socks, water bottles and boot-liners in her sleeping bag. The next day the group split into two rope teams of four and began to ferry food, fuel and gear down Heartbreak Hill then up through a large crevasse field to the first cache. An inch shy of five feet and weighing 90 pounds, Merrick carried a 60-pound pack in addition to pulling a sled. It was a slog, hauling supplies on the top-heavy plastic sleds. It was also HOT!

Avalanche sweeps towards base camp at Kahiltna Glacier.

Dehydration is a problem, so you have to drink a lot of water, which leads to another problem. Unzipping and squatting are out of the question so Merrick brought along a Lady Jane--a plastic cup with a tube she calls a "wannabe"--in other words, now she could pee standing up!

Day 3 June 4

Blue skies. Sunny. This is spring skiing weather. Merrick yearns to go snowboarding in "sun city" --instead she helps set up camp in what her mother calls "the most beautiful place in the world." The camp at 7800' is across from the crevasse field of the Northeast Fork known as the Valley of Death. Avalanches sweep down from Windy Corner and sweep away anything in their path. The sun and snow pose a real hazard of sunburn. Merrick reapplied sunscreen every five minutes. A bandana protected her

Dug in and set up at Base Camp. Denali is framed in the background.

The Acey Deucys: J.T.Lindholm, Jennifer Johnston (otherwise known as 'Mom,')Steve Young, Jani Oviatte, Breck Eagle, Merrick Johnston,Chuck Landry and Danielle Carvalho.

neck but reflected sun quickly burned the bottom of her tongue and the roof of her mouth.

As climbers moved supplies up the mountain, underneath their feet the Kahiltna Glacier grinds along, opening deep blue rifts called crevasses. Merrick had fun lowering herself into the mouth of these eerie blue holes. Beneath the surface she hung, suspended by thin rope, listening to the echoing sounds of the ice.

That night, snug in her sleeping bag, Merrick pulled out a small yellow weatherproof journal. In the front is a date and a dedication:

**20 May 1995
from
Norman and Carolyn Vaughan
"Far better it is to dare mighty things, to win glorious triumphs, even though checkered by failure, than to take rank with those poor souls who neither enjoy much or suffer much, because they live in the gray twilight that knows not victory nor defeat."**

Theodore Roosevelt 1899

Two days before she left to climb Denali, Norman had given Merrick the journal, an Explorer's Club flag and a small red rock chipped from the summit of Mt. Vaughan, a peak in the Queen Maude Mountains of Antarctica. She carried all three items in her pack.

L ate at night the mountain brings music to the camp. Big rumbling snowfalls cascade down the glacier, the ice cracks and the swishing sound of air and great volumes of moving snow give an edge to sleep. Breakfast is bagels, peanut butter and honey and hot cereal. Merrick spends most of her down time playing rummy, cribbage, backgammon, and hearts. "Games are my life," she said with a grin, explaining she takes after an uncle who is card player in Costa Rica.

The team roped up and left the cache around 5 p.m. after the weather cleared. Merrick led. She set a fast pace, sweating a bit on the steep pitches. The wind came up as they reached the ridge, but Merrick didn't stop to put on her parka because they were so close to camp. Ten minutes later she was dragging, teary-eyed and in the first stages of hypothermia. Jennifer stopped and helped her get into her warm mittens and jacket. It was a long, cold fifteen minutes to camp. Her mother got her in the tent and in her sleeping bag and cuddled with her.

"It seemed like we were ten feet from camp but it was hard for me to walk," she said later. "I didn't know if I was gonna make it. I was really cold but I was hot. I felt like I was ice. I'd never felt like that before. I couldn't think. I just wanted to go to sleep." Merrick was embarrassed but she had learned a hard lesson the easy way. Next time she would stop and put on another layer. In a half hour, her body temperature back to normal, she was up laughing and singing in the cook tent.

Merrick's Journal-Day 3
I haven't written in this thing yet, because not enough time. I'll give you a summary. I've been stuck next to J.T. on the rope. Usually he doesn't stop farting. I'm writing this at 7800 feet. I enjoy spending time together the most. I really like Vernon's group, especially Marty. He's real funny. He plays a guitar real well. Vernon plays the harmonica and fiddle. I love singing. Marty doesn't laugh; he eats chili. I hate dried milk. I like my group.

Day 5-June 6
The A.D.'s moved their cache to 9700 feet. It was a heavy three-mile carry up Ski Hill. Merrick and J.T. led, singing songs the whole way. The 12,525 foot Kahiltna Dome rose on the left, the West Rim of Denali on the right. Skiers and climbers passed them on the way down. Unroped and unconcerned, they skidded by on their plastic sleds. Steve insisted on ropes and snowshoes. The area was riddled with crevasses. At any point an ice bridge could collapse, taking whomever happened to be on it on their last wild ride.

Dinner is served at 16200 feet by Steve Young and Merrick. Kitchen is at the face of the headwall.

Merrick's Journal
I love dining. It is fun, no worries, no pain, just fun. It is snowing wet snow. I played a game of acey deucy with J.T. and Breck. I beat them both. I'm winning in hearts right now. My tongue hurts, it is burnt. I think J.T. and my mom farted about 1,000,000 times in the tent. It stinks bad. I forgot to take my pulse this morning. My mom farted again. J.T. drools on other people's stuff.

High wispy clouds swept across Denali and Foraker. At first just thin frothy wisps, in an hour they became wind-whipped clouds, that descended in a thick wet layer on camp. At 9700 feet it took three hours to shovel out a camp site.

Merrick's job from Day 1 was to build the bathrooms. On the mountain, climbers pee in a hole but poop in a bag. The bag is then tossed down a deep crevasse. The job is an important one because all drinking water comes from melted snow and contaminated snow has made many climbers sick--some too sick to summit. Merrick's first privy was an interesting one. It had a spectacular view and a magazine rack but the pee hole was a good five feet from the poop bag. This made moving from one to another pretty difficult. Next time she got it right.

The winds howled and the snow dumped and the climbers had to dig themselves out at 3 a.m. and again at 6 a.m. Another day pinned down by weather, or if you looked at it from Merrick's point of view, another day to visit with friends, play hearts and beat the pants off everyone in the tent. By 5 p.m. the weather is clearing and dinner is served: Grits with bacon bits and cheese! An hour later the ferry to 11,000 feet begins.

Merrick's Journal
I got a little bit hypothermic last night, while we were getting the cache. I wasn't having much fun. This morning I was sleeping in everything. It was about 100 degrees. J.T. peed 1 1/2 quarts in one shot. Hc has the bladder of a cow. We got to sleep at 4:00 a.m. and woke at 9:00 I got only 5 hours of sleep. I have a bloody cut on my finger. It won't heal. We cached at 9700'. I led both ways. I beat J.T. at cribbage and rummy. I haven't lost a game yet.

Note: This was Merrick's last journal entry. From here on her journal became the score book for games and she kept the team's daily pulse rate.

"One reason I climbed the mountain was so my older brother would talk to me," Merrick said.

Steve set a blistering pace and didn't seem to notice when the climbers behind him wanted to stop. Merrick was struggling. Her chapstick/jack-knife cord was wrapped around her neck and she was choking. Each step her mother took pulled the rope and harness and cord tighter. "We were sweating and my legs felt like jelly," Merrick recalled. "I couldn't call out because we were in a storm. No one heard me. It was awful."

When Steve finally stopped Breck moved forward and untangled Merrick's cord. Next on the rope was a scared mom. "I heard Merrick crying behind me," Jennifer said. "I couldn't begin to guess how she felt."

At 10,500 feet the sky cleared to a deep blue and the snow was tinged with gold. The team reached the cache, unloaded, roped up and Merrick led the way down. In camp by midnight they had hot soup and a meeting to hash over what had gone wrong. Steve said when it was time to go it was time to go: Merrick was fooling around playing games instead of packing up. J.T. and Jennifer told Steve they were disappointed he did not stop for a rest. He said they did not communicate their problems well. Finally the air was cleared. Back in the tent Merrick promised her mother she would work harder and do better next time. The next day Acey Deucy was a tighter team.

"I didn't know if I wanted to keep going if it would all be like that," Merrick said after she was almost strangled by her cord.

Day 8 June 9

Sunny skies again. Kahiltna Pass at 11,200 feet is blue. Blue ice, blue snow, blue clouds and sky. Huge seracs hang from the ridges. To the left of the basin is a monster crevasse. The camp is a party town. Merrick hangs out with the Hanson girls; three sisters who are climbing with their father. Nicole hopes to be the youngest girl, at 15, to ever summit. She and Merrick play cards with the park rangers. Both girls cheat.

Merrick builds the camp privy with a great view, but puts the pee hole at the bottom of a steep pitch. That night in a storm she has her big brush with death. Unroped, in a whiteout, she races out of the tent between card games on her way to the privy. And she falls.

In a mere second her life changes--from carefree to desperate-- as she slides down; down toward a cornice of snow and a 3000 foot vertical drop. She is accelerating, trying to stab her boots tips into the ice, when she grabs something embedded alongside the trail. Her mother's ice axe has saved her from a long drop and a sudden death.

Day 9 June 10

Motorcycle Hill made us feel like mountaineers, Jennifer remembered. "It was blowing to beat the band. We hunkered in behind some rocks, put on another layer, and waited for the second rope team.

Steve put in a ice picket for the climbers to hook into as they traversed the ice field. It is a 3000 foot drop to Peter's Basin. Then they were off to Windy Corner. Steve tied Merrick closer to him. It was here where three men from Washington died a few weeks earlier when the ice bridge they were on collapsed crushing them to death.

While Merrick is on Denali she will see death but she will also see some of the causes: "Death is short on Denali. You are pitting your knowlege and your physical skills against the mountain," she explained later from the safety of her living room in Anchorage. "The people who die choose to be there. And they made mistakes. It's kind of like when my mom tells me not to do something and I do it and I get hurt--she won't feel sorry for me. That's sort of the way it is on McKinley. When someone dies it's their decision. It's really sad once you get down here though, but it's a whole different world up there. It's just a big white place where you really have to concentrate on what you are doing...on yourself. On survival."

Day 10 June 11

Camp is moved to McKinley City at 14,300 feet. The wind blows so hard here Merrick thinks she can fly. J.T. is excited to learn that prunes come from plums. He eats at least 25 prunes and the next day when he thinks he's dying, Jennifer reminds him of the prunes. He is relieved that it isn't high atltitude sickness, but his condition is hard on his other tent mates.

Climbing from 11,000 feet to 14,300 feet took ten hours. At one point the team passes four climbers coming down. The group didn't make the top but they didn't care. They were all smiles. One guy had tried to summit five times, for five years. Never made it, but no worries. He was coming back. He loved this place.

At 14,300 feet it was party central, with close to 100 climbers dug in at McKinley City. Merrick had made her first fundraising goal. The higher she got the more sponsors had pledged money to a family wellness agency.

Day 12 June 13

With each step Merrick sunk in thick snow. When a climber reached a ice bridge they yelled "CREVASSE!" Once a climber was safely over they yelled "ACROSS!" This kept everyone on the rope on their toes. Ferrying a load to 16,200 feet there is a 1000 foot stretch with a 45 degree pitch up the headwall.

Denali-and the Alaska Range foothills. A Southside view .

On a clear day, at this level, climbers can see forever: the green and brown of the tundra on one side, the white and blue of the Alaska Range on the other. Merrick dug out a snow cave--she looked like a marmot wriggling into the powder.

Day 14-15

Rest days. The team needed time to acclimate to the attitude. High air made some people "get real weird," Merrick remembers. "I think it's a combination of altitude and fear. People realize they have been kidding themselves about their ability." She spent much of the time listening closely to reports of a Taiwanese group that was in trouble. Three of the men had stumbled into a camp at 17,200 feet and five were missing. Weather had closed in around seven of them on the summit. As the day progressed the news was better. Seven of them were alive. Of the three who wandered in a storm on a flat plateau called the Football Field, two were alive. They had survived horrendous winds and temperatures. Their hands and feet were frozen blocks of ice.The third was dead.

Day15-16

Weather is bad. The climbers don't move except to move the card playing party to the boy's tent.

Day 17 June 18

Camp was moved to 16,100 feet. It still took a while to pack up. Mountaineering is a system of lists, layers, and straps. Liner soles, liner socks, outer socks, and liner boots fit into plastic boots. There are longjohns, layers of fleece, inner gloves, and outer Gortex. Crampons, harnesses, poles, and ice axes all have straps. There are ropes to put on, pack, or carry. Then there's the pack. Foam pads, sleeping bag, water bottles, parka, head- hand- and foot-gear, cards and books!

Merrick and Breck spent three hours digging out a snowcave. Later, in their sleeping bags, Breck pulled out a book of poetry and ballads and each climber took a turn reading. Merrick and her mom went to bed discussing whether it was better to go to sleep with your socks on or off. Merrick says off; Jennifer says on. Jennifer's feet stay warm but sometimes her socks

aren't dry in the morning. Merrick's feet are cold at first but warm up later, and she always has dry socks in the morning. Neither can see the other's point of view.

High camp at 17,200 feet reminds everyone that a summit try is in the near future. Climbing the narrow West Buttress ridge with a 2000 foot drop on each side reminds Merrick of the beam work she did in gymnastics.

Except "sometimes it was even narrower than the beam," she shuddered. Ahead is Washburn's Thumb, named for Brad Washburn, the climber who pioneered the West Buttress route with his wife Barbara in 1952. Also in view is Denali's black-rock north peak. This was the site of a notorious 1910 climb by a group of sourdoughs from Fairbanks who carried a spruce tree with them and stuck it in the snow on top in case anyone doubted they had been there. Danielle and Jani suffer from the altitude. They have bad headaches. Steve lays out their options over hot ramen noodle soup, red beans and rice, hot cocoa, and nutter butters.

The whole team is not ready for a summit attempt but the weather is good. Should the teams split up and go for the summit separately?

"No way!" said J.T.

Danielle agreed. Steve, Breck and Chuck want to wait and see. Merrick and Jennifer decide four people at the top would be kind of lonely. Soon the decision is made. The A.D.'s are a team. They go together.

Day 18-19 June 19

Beautiful day. No wind. The Hansons and Vernon Tejas' group have gone for the summit. The Acey Deucy's spend the day regrouping.

Everyone is back in camp by midnight. Tiffany Hanson made the summit and is for now the youngest woman to have climbed Denali. Merrick is happy for her.

Days 20-23 June 21

Bad weather kept the climbers in camp in their tents. The winds slam down the mountain. The longer the climbers stay pinned down, the more used to the altitude they become. That's the good part. The down side is the longer they stay, the more likely they will run out of food before they can make a summit attempt.

Merrick and Steve build an igloo over the privy to kill time and spend the rest of the day carving ice blocks to shore up the snow walls that protect the tents. J.T. told a whole bunch of terrible jokes (this is not as easy as it sounds because breathing is real hard at this altitude) and just when the rest of the team was ready to cut off his air completely, the sky opened up and there was Archdeacon's Tower (19,200 feet.) The tower was named after Episcopal Archdeacon of the Yukon, Hudson Stuck. But Stuck was not stuck in church all the time. He led the first ascent of the south summit of Denali in 1913. He was joined by Walter Harper, an Alaskan Native, Harry Karstens, and Robert Tatum.

Now the A.C. team set off across The Football Field, just 800 feet shy of the summit ridge. This is it!

Merrick was in the lead. Every step in this thin air is hard. To keep going Merrick counted to 1000. "Then I would sing," she said. She also pictured herself on the summit. Imagined finishing it. Step, lock the knee, rest. Swing the ice axe for another, higher bite. Step, lock, rest. Step, lock, rest.

The snow reflected the golden light of dusk in the Land of the Midnight Sun. It was 10:30 p.m. when Merrick stepped onto the summit ridge. The two teams combined, with Chuck in the lead and Merrick and her mother right behind him. On one side the drop off was steep, well over 7000 feet; on the other side the pitch was 1000 feet.

Merrick's gymnastics experience on the balance beam kept her calm. "It started out cloudy but 200 feet from the top we broke out of the clouds and it was all pink! Everything! It was really pretty. We could see for a hundred miles. The sun was orange and the clouds were pink and the shadow of McKinley was dark blue on those pink clouds. It was a Kodak moment!"

Merrick's moment at the top of the world lasted 20 minutes. So what does it all mean?

As the pink light washed over the summit Merrick realized she had grown. "I learned I could always finish everything I started as long as it was within my capabilities. Like if we are doing a 70 mile hike I could finish as long as I thought about it. I learned to cooperate and communicate. I know I won't be able to do some things on my first try...but you can do anything you want if you just take the time and think about it." Merrick wanted to try Denali on for size. Now, with Denali behind her, Merrick has her sights set on seventh grade and Mt. Vinson in the Antarctic. Yes, she wants to go to the land of Mt. Vaughan because she says, she finally understands what the dedication Norman wrote in her journal means.

"Far better it is to dare mighty things...."

"I thought about Norman a lot up there," she recalled as she sat curled in a ball on the living room couch on a late December morning. "I wished he was on Denali with me. I wished I known him when he was 12. It would be really weird. I had the rock he gave me all the

way to the top. Now he's got to take it somewhere. We are just going to pass it back and forth." Both adventurers have plans. Norman is going to the North Pole next. And Merrick?

She wants to do it all.

**Chuck, Merrick, Jani and Jennifer on the Summit Ridge.
Right; Steve, Merrick and Jennifer whoop it up!**

The team moves along the knife ridge below Camp Crockett. "He never gives up," Carolyn marveled. "Can't is not a word in his vocabulary."

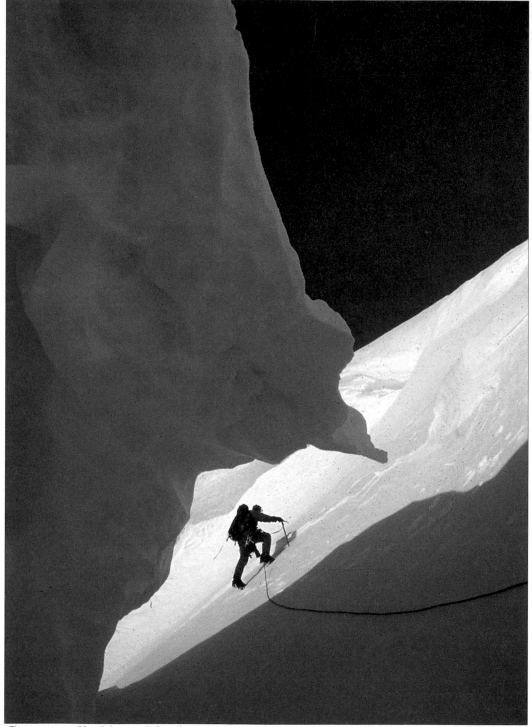

B yrd called us the Three Musketeers. Eddie, Freddie and me. They're both dead now but I feel close to them here. Like both of them are with me, watching me. Once, near here, Eddie pulled me from a crevasse. It was Freddie's idea to hook Rex and Fido to our Flexible Flyer sled when we were both 12. We had been reading a book about Eskimos and made our harnesses from rope. When we yelled Mush! both dogs turned and jumped in our laps. "

Step. Lock. Wait.
Step. Lock. Wait.

Camp Goodale at 7300 feet is named after Eddie. When Norman reaches Camp Crockett he is snowblind with a painful sunburn of the retinas. He spends the next two days in a sleeping bag with his eyes shut. Outside the thin nylon tent the temperature is 40 below zero.

December 6

When the team sets out again Norman is struggling. Wind rakes the mountain. For the old explorer it is one foot in front of the other, again and again; for Vernon and Gordon--climbers at the peak of their ability--it is a challenge to move slowly and to be patient. By the time they reach the top they will have chopped over 320 footholds in the snow. That night they have made it another 500 hundred feet to Camp Gould . Norman must spend another night. He is completely exhausted. But the weather is going bad and the next morning the team decides to push for the summit.

Crevasse climbing, altitude and age take a toll on the old explorer, right.

There's a whole lot of smooching going on! At the top Norman and Carolyn plant one on Vernon's head. Three days shy of his 89th birthday, Carolyn christens the mountain as cake; the snow: frosting and the 89 sparklers from her pack: the candles. Norman carried 'Zippy' to the top to honor the brave dogs of Antarctica.

One hundred feet from the top Vaughan takes the lead. At a brown craggy outcropping of stone they pause and Vernon chips several chunks loose with his ice axe. Norman slips one small piece into his pocket.

Step. Lock. Rest.

"I can't believe it," Norman roars as he crests the mountain and surveys the view from the bottom of the world. "Everywhere you look...it's tremendous!" Mount Vaughan has finally met its match. Norman's words are carried on a bone-chilling wind across an ice-covered continent.

"Dream big! Young and old!" he shouts. "Dream big and dare to fail!"

Vernon Tejas fiddles a tune.

December 4 1994

Base Camp deGanahl--named for Joe deGanahl, another Byrd dog driver--was set at 6700 feet. That left 3600 feet of mountain to go. There was nothing here but ice and snow and rock. The air is so clear the distant peaks dance on the horizon 100 miles away. The color of the Antarctic is cold blue. Nose hairs quickly stiffen with frost and the dry air cuts at the throat.

> "I know how to dream big dreams. But Norman dreams impossible dreams. That's what I want to learn from him."
>
> Vernon Tejas

Norman led out of camp but after only a few feet he must shed his pack. Vern and Gordon begin to chop and kick steps in the snow. Sixty five years ago, when he was a young man of 23, Norman could have run up this mountain in ten hours. Now, thanks to a pair of frozen feet he got in the Iditarod, he can't feel the steps he takes. It makes keeping his balance on the steep slope hard.

Step. Lock. Wait.
Step. Lock. Wait.

Norman can't look up and enjoy the view. He must concentrate on his feet. Willing them to lift. Kick. Steady. They stop every few minutes for a pulse check. Since he can't look around Norman looks inside instead.

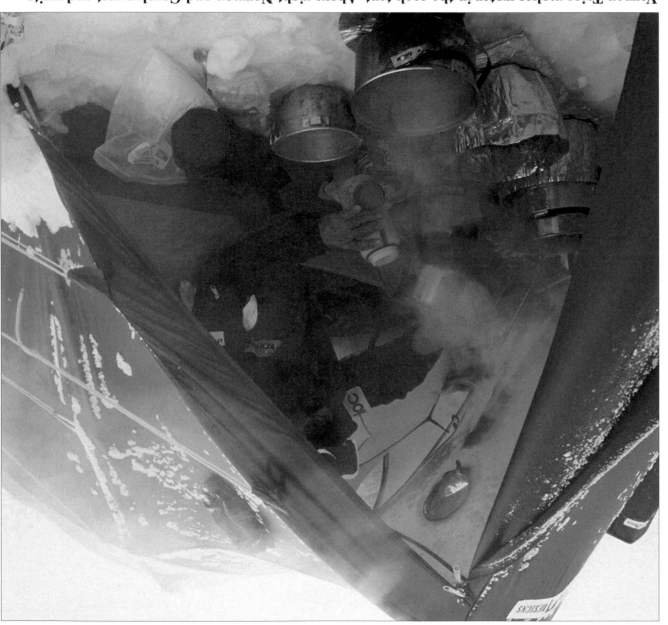

N orman, Carolyn, renowned Alaskan climber Vernon Tejas and mountaineer photographer Gordon Wiltsie will make the next attempt. Norman practiced self-arrest techniques in case of a fall. Norman learned to pull himself from a crevasse and how to kick the toe of his boot into the snow with each step. He spends hour after hour on the treadmill and climbing the stairs wearing a 70 lb. pack.

Step. Lock. Wait.
Step. Lock. Wait.

December 3 1994

"We arrived by airplane at the base of Mount Vaughan. Flying in we looked out of the window and suddenly there it was! I couldn't believe it! Something I had thought of, dreamed of for 65 years. My heart was in my throat. It was different than the photos I had seen. It had looked small. Now it stuck 10,302 feet into the sky. It just looked tremendous!"

Vernon Tejas makes water in the cook tent. Above right Norman and Carolyn rest and write.

Things are looking up!! Carolyn and Norman survey his peak.

Step. Lock. Wait.
Step. Lock. Wait.
He practiced his climbing technique on the seven flights of stairs in the hotel at Punta Arenas, Chile.

Step. Lock. Wait.
Step. Lock. Wait.

His heart and his head screamed, "I'm young!!" but his body seem to have a hard time hearing them. His ankle is shot and his knee is made of plastic. It makes him stumble a lot.

It took a year and another $250,000 before the team would make another attempt. And this time the dogs would have to stay home.

"We had wanted to pay tribute to all the brave dogs that made exploration to the poles possible," Norman said. "I would have been the first and the last American to drive dogs on the Antarctic continent."

It was a bittersweet decision to consider an adventure to the Antarctic without dogs. But the goal was the summit of Mount Vaughan and Norman has always put the goal first.

> "So much of his life has depended on never losing sight of the goal. Of course most people will discourage you; it is a rare person who has both the courage and vision to act. Norman always figured he could get around roadblocks by looking for another route."
>
> Carolyn Muegge Vaughan

- In 1932 he raced a dog team in the Olympics at Lake Placid, New York.
- During World War II Vaughan was in charge of Search and Rescue for the North Atlantic Fleet. He devised a plan to rescue wounded soldiers during the Battle of the Bulge using sled dogs. He planned to drop them out of airplanes using doggy parachutes!
- He skied, played polo, wrote books , broke the world record for long distance snowmobile travel driving from Anchorage, Alaska to Boston. And he became bored with his life in the East.
- In 1974 he moved to Alaska and started over. There the 1049 mile Iditarod Sled Dog Race became the focus of his life.

"My parents wanted me to lead a proper life. They were very particular about how I acted. But I couldn't imagine staying in New Hampshire and selling Vaughan's Ivory Shoe Leather in the family business. It would have been duller than dish water. I think one should be true to his nature. I was a failure in my father's eyes because I didn't earn any money. But not in my eyes. I have not failed myself. If I was to live life over again I think I would be just as curious- to do those crazy things all over again just the same."

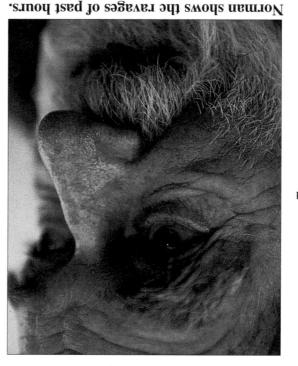

Norman shows the ravages of past hours.

"Go get your mountain, buddy."

Jerry Vanek from his hospital bed

"I wanted to be different. I wanted to be a leader," Norman said. His leadership skills were put to the test after the supply plane crashed.

"I was so excited," Norman remembered as he watched the supply plane take off. "The Mount Vaughan Expedition--the first expedition with my name in it--was off to a good start. After so much hard work and frustration I went to bed a happy man."

Less than eight hours later Norman's dream had turned into a night-mare. The supply plane had crashed six miles short of the runway at Patriot Hills. The expedition veterinarian, Jerry Vanek, was critically injured and four dogs were lost. Retrieving supplies was out of the question. Spending the rest of the expedition funds to rescue Vanek and the dogs was imperative.

That night, as Norman sat in tears with his team members, it looked as if the Mount Vaughan Expedition had failed. Jerry's bloodied and bruised body, his shattered leg and gruesome head injuries had shaken them all. "I brought all these people down here," Norman said, his head in his hands. "It's a helluva responsibility." Yet he didn't give up.

The Mount Vaughan Expedition gets underway with Vernon in lead. At right, Carolyn Vaughan communicates with students who are following the climb via the Internet.

the Antarctic on Thanksgiving Day 1993.

It was a crazy match. Carolyn Muegge was 36 years younger than Norman. Just for the fun of it she'd come to his home in Alaska to help with his dog team for the 1986 Iditarod Sled Dog Race. But Carolyn shared Norman's love of adventure and soon she shared his dream too. Together they took the first steps toward the big adventure at the bottom of the world.

"I am a dreamer; Carolyn is an organizer. Together we made a plan. First we needed to raise money--more than a million dollars--to transport dogs and supplies to base camp. We planned to drive dogs over the same terrain we explored with dogs 65 years earlier," Norman said.

The money was hard to come by, but finally--just a few short months shy of a deadline banning dogs from the Antarctic--a plane filled with supplies, 20 huskies and team members took off from Punta Arenas, Chili, bound for the Antarctic on Thanksgiving Day 1993.

Vaughan practices arresting a fall prior to the climb.

F or sixty-five years Norman Vaughan dreamed of his mountain. "I kept thinking that somehow I could get back down there." The bottom of the world haunted him and his "regular" life seemed pale and empty. "We were closer to God on that trip," he explained, recalling the near disasters in crevasse fields, the winds that could freeze flesh in seconds and storms that could sweep sleds sideways into the sea. "We realized how insignificant we humans really were!"

"Some people may perceive the things that I do as a risk but I have learned how to do bold things in my life and now I am only matching the challenge to my abilities."

As the years passed the Antarctic seemed to drift farther away and his dream became as distant as Mount Vaughan's fog shrouded peak. Then at an age when most men are falling over dead, Norman fell in love.

After Byrd's successful flight over the South Pole he named three peaks in the Queen Maude Mountains in honor of his "Three Musketeers," Vaughan, Goodale and Crockett. When Norman got the news he was delighted. "Gosh, that's great, Commander! I'll have to go back and climb mine."

"I bet you will," Admiral Byrd said.

The young men had come of age on the ice, toughened by wind and tempered by cold. They had been tested and all three had come up winners. Norman remembers the last day on the ice when Byrd lowered the American flag for the final time and turned to shake his hand. "We did it," was all the Commander said.

Admiral Byrd just before the flight to the South Pole. He is holding the flag and a stone from the grave of Floyd Bennet. The flag and stone were dropped at the Pole.

Pilots like Charles Lindberg were national heroes and Byrd's aviation expedition captured the imagination of the world.

The men used their dog teams to drag Byrd's Ford Trimotor airplane to safe ice and there, at a site later dubbed Little America, they built a city under the snow. It would be their home through the six months of winter darkness when temperatures plummeted to 73 degrees below zero. In the spring of 1929 Freddie, Eddie and Norman were part of a team that covered 1500 miles on a geological survey. Traveling with the dogs, they surveyed the Queen Maude Mountains, exploring lands that had never before been seen by man.

"I was thrilled the whole time I was down there," Norman remembers. "We were walking in the steps of heroes-- Shackleton, Peary, Amundsen--and we were making new tracks of our own."

Norman sailed to Antarctica on a tall ship called 'The City of New York.' They spent the winter night on the Ross Ice Shelf-the exact camp has long since broken off and drifted out to sea. To the dismay of their parents, Eddie Goodale and Norman's other buddy, Freddie Crockett went along. They were the expedition dog handlers and Byrd called them his 'Three Musketeers.'

Byrd's goal was to be the first to fly over the South Pole. He needed men on the ground in the event he was forced down or had to crash. Norman was one of those men.

Many people think spending two years at the bottom of the world--in the bleak and barren heart of the Antarctic--would be misery beyond belief. For Norman the blue ice was paradise. He loved it.

While others reeled from the crash of the stock market back in America, Norman and his two best friends, Eddie Goodale and Freddie Crockett, spent the first weeks of the Antarctic summer of 1928 helping move 650 tons of supplies by dog team into the interior. In those days--the last days of the great explorers--sending a team to the South Pole was as daunting as, well, sending a man to the moon.

Above: As part of the 1928 Byrd Expedition to the South Pole the scientific party under direction of Laurence Gould of the National Science Foundation spent months exploring the continent. "It was during this trip through the Queen Maude Mountains that I saw the peak that would one day bear my name. I promised myself then that some day, some how I would come back and climb it," said Vaughan. Left-Vaughan at 23, Antarctica bound.

Explorer Norman Vaughan, age 89, gets a look at Mount Vaughan.

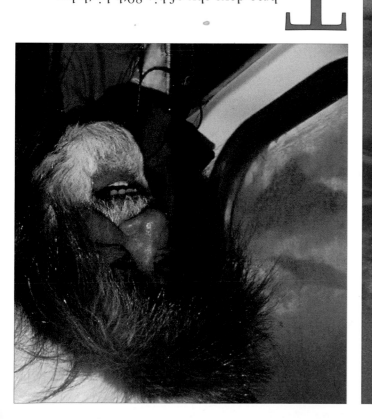

Three days shy of his 89th birthday Norman Vaughan stood on top of a mountain at the bottom of the world. He had never climbed a mountain before, but this one was special. This one was named after him. Imagine: a piece of the planet with your name on it. This 10,302 foot granite rock is called Mount Vaughan. It sits in the midst of the coldest, windiest, most hostile place in the world. Antarctica.

The peak was named by Admiral Richard E. Byrd, commander of the first American expedition to the South Pole. Norman was a sophomore at Harvard when he read the headlines of the newspaper: BYRD TO THE POLE! "It was as if an electrical bolt ran up my spine," he recalled. "I just had to take part in the adventure of the century!"

For kids who dream of far off places;
who see themselves as heroes in this amazing dance of life.
And of course especially to Kye;
whose name means 'the spirit of life!'

ADVENTURE AT THE TOP OF THE WORLD/
ADVENTURE AT THE BOTTOM OF THE WORLD

By SHELLEY GILL
Photos by GORDON WILTSIE, J.T. LINDHOLM, JENNIFER JOHNSTON
Text copyright © Shelley Gill 1996
Photos copyright © Gordon Wiltsie J.T. Lindholm, Jennifer Johnston1996
PAWS IV PUBLISHING
P.O. Box 2364
Homer, Alaska 99603
To order call 1-800-807-PAWS
Library of Congress Number 96-67615
ISBN (pb) 0-934007-28-4
ISBN (hb) 0-934007-30-6
First Edition 1996
Printed in the United States on recycled paper

89 year-old explorer Norman Vaughan revisits the Queen
Maude Mountains in Antarctica to climb the mountain named
for him by Admiral Richard E. Byrd.
12 year-old adventurer Merrick Johnston becomes the youngest
person to ever scale Denali--North America's highest peak.

ADVENTURE AT THE BOTTOM
OF THE WORLD

By SHELLEY GILL
Photos by GORDON WILTSIE